AN

A LITTLE BIT

MORE!

A second collection of poems by

AngieD

Thanks again to God. This second book is dedicated to my mother and her best friend - Aunt Barbara; I can almost hear them both giggling away, and to Uncle Ken. Also to Mother Mac, Uncle Les and Aunt Enid.   For all their help over the years – my very grateful thanks.

May they all rest in peace.

FOREWORD

And, so, another year, what has changed —
not much — the world remains imperfect.
We live in a damaged world, I am not
spotless, who is? So, yes, things still go wrong
every day, but life continues and through it all
we must learn — I must learn - to work at it
with a smile.

I remain hopeful something in here will
conjure up a smile from a reader!

Fingers crossed!

AngieD

Coming UP

Worry not of my faux pas –
I'm only human - oops!   11

The Pleasures of travel –
(Can't help but see what's in front of me!)   47

One of the many wonders of our land –
(Beauty in petals)   59

Hospitaloscopy of life Pt1 – A stick up!   67

The romance – Let's get loving   71

The weighting game   83

Hospitaloscopy of life Pt2
Bedside prep for photoshoot!   99

Revival Time – Let's lay back and chill   101

Hospitaloscopy of life Pt3
The photo finish!   109

What's in a year?   111

Apres Christmas   135

First encounters of the four-legged kind   143

Our ever changing world – or not!   151

The year that was (2022) –   159

In what/who do I trust....   177

Feeling the blues - music's the clue!   187

And so..let life continue!   203

WORRY NOT OF MY FAUX PAS – I'M HUMAN! - OOPS!

DRESSED IN FOOD!

I used to regard myself
As a tidy eater
But am beginning to change my view
'Cause snacking in front of the tv
My suspicions quickly grew

Whether it falls from the fork
Or misses my mouth
Requires further investigation
But remains on my clothes that travel south
Is definitely proof of lack of concentration!

My washing machine
Has its work cut out
From ketchup that missed its chips
To spinach and gooey melted cheese
That continues to miss my lips!

There are only two solutions
That I can see
And, though I'm a long time out of my crib
But either I sit at the table and eat my food
Or resort to wearing a bib!

LUCKY TRIPS!

I've tripped, but not fallen
Twice already
I've not been drinking
So, why am I unsteady?

I pay great attention
T'where I place my feet
'Cause I know pavements are uneven
On road and street

Perhaps it's those bright lights
Of cars blinding the view
From my perfect eyes
Down to my shoe

I'm not sure the reason
But I'd better find out soon
Before my nose hits the ground
And swells up like a balloon!

PARANOIA!

I was happy, healthy
And content
Kept a check
On money spent

That is until I watched tv
Now every ache felt and blemish I see
The ads have me wondering
What's wrong with me?

According to them
My hair's too thin
So need an expensive conditioner 'nd shampoo
To massage and leave in

My face needs a pick-me-up
It's looking tragic
And needs regular botox
To work its magic

If I'm a little sad
Or feeling low
It's therapy I need
To maintain that glow

That vital refreshing
Feng shui feeling
Is what my house needs to make it
More appealing

If something angers
Or irritates
I obviously need counselling
To regain a calm state

Hmmm!
They'll soon have me convinced
That I'm way off track
My gait is all wrong
And that I walk front to back!

PAINFUL PRICK!

I could sit all day
Watching swimmers in the sea
If they like cold salty water – fine for them
But it's not for me!

The thought of jellyfish and other stuff
That lurk deep down
Makes me certain that I'm safer
On firm ground

But sometimes I wonder
Is it really better on sand
Where particles stick to bits
Other than your hand

And with creatures with pincers
Eager to feed
Dry land may be more painful
Than harmless seaweed

When I was last at the beach
Though it wasn't particularly hot
An uncomfortable case of prickly heat
Was all I got!

SUCH A LOSER!

Now, I've lost a hankie
Last week it was a sock
But I've been searching for my hankie
Since five o'clock

I took it out my coat pocket
When I came in last night
And between then and this morning
It's nowhere in sight

I do have lots more
All brand new
But as I take one out
I lose that too

I'm not sure of the solution
Except to adhere
A corner of my hankie
To the lobe of my left ear!

NOT A CHANCE TO DANCE!

I went dancing last Saturday
A lovely affair
The room was packed
And excitement filled the air

The bar had a queue -
We all wanted drinks
A colourful atmosphere girls dressed in
Reds, blues and pinks

The band was introduced
Then started to play
And everyone was smiling
As they began to sway

Then some guests got up
And headed for the floor
First a couple
Then came more

Wriggling around
Dancing along
Some were even singing
'Cause they knew the song

I was ready to join them
To bop to the beat
But as I changed my shoes I realised
I had brought two left feet!

EAR EAR!

I think my ears are getting smaller
'Cause my sunglasses keep falling off
They used to stay on if I moved my head
Or if I sneezed or started to cough

But now when I put them on
The left side can't seem to find
A big enough part of my left ear
To stick its arm behind

It falls off onto my shoulder
While the right one stays in place
And I feel as though I'm walking around
With a very lopsided face

I'm between a rock and that hard place
Of where I go from here
Either shave a bit off the right one to even it
up
Or stay with my little left ear!

EAT THYSELF!

You don't realise how sharp your teeth are
Until you accidentally grip
And feel excruciating pain when you discover
You've not chewed your food but y'lip

You can do nothing
But bear the pain
And chew slowly so one doesn't
Bite the same place again

It's now not a matter of enjoying
The meal you've begun
But ensuring you don't consume
Either your lip or your tongue!

TWO-FACED!

Ouch! Something went and bit me
On my face
Why did they pick
Such a conspicuous place

Now I've a zit
Large and red
Almost resembling
A second head!

Why could it not have chosen
A leg or an arm
And so cause no embarrassment
Or psychological harm

I can't even hide it
Under a scarf
I'm just praying no one notices
And begins to laugh

They say toothpaste is good
For menacing spots
So, for now I'll have to walk round with
A face with a large white dot!

JUST PANTS!

Have you ever tried to walk
With y'trousers falling down
And you can't do anything about it
Being far from shop and out of town

When I wore my leggings last time
The elastic in my waist was fine
It held my assets up marvelously
Like cork in a bottle of wine

But if you'd seen me on my stroll
Placing each step with care
Trying to keep my "asset holder" up
So as not to show my wares

You'd be forgiven for thinking
I was off course
And that somewhere along the way
I'd gone and lost my horse!

How I wish I'd travelled by car
Instead of on the train
Then I wouldn't be in this predicament
Trying to keep my dignity and hiding my shame!

SKIN 'N' BONE!

I was cutting up a chicken leg the other day
And thought, "My, my!"
This is small – where are the big ones
My mother used to buy?

The ones that when put on your plate
Took up half the room
And was so big it took most of
The dinner time to consume

Modern day chickens
As far as I can see
Appear like the model size zero
The authorities want us all to be

Less flesh more bone
And way way too thin
One can't even compensate for lack of meat
By eating the yummy crispy skin

Not sure what they're given
At mealtimes to eat
Perhaps they need a bowl or two
Of breakfast cereal wheat!

If evolution and society
Intervene any more
It won't be chicken meat we'll be eating
But feathers, beak and claw!

FLIGHT INVASION!

It should've passed by
But it flew up my nose
Sometimes I wish nostrils had shutters
That would automatically close

When anything came within
Five inches of my face
Sensors would be activated
To shut down that space

I wonder where in my stomach it is
And what it's doing
Is it eating the food
I'm daily chewing?

Was it an 'ermaphrodite
And this daddy and mummy
Was producing kids
Inside my tummy

Are the inner rumblings I feel
Them flying about
Playing with their siblings
Or trying to get out?

Should I go to the surgery
And say " doctor - I've swallowed a fly
It was unavoidable
I was just walking by

We were in the same area
At the same time
Its body came into contact
And flew into mine"!

Was it blind?
I'm big enough to see
Who's at fault - must've been them
'Cause it definitely wasn't me

So, if you see me and I appear irrational
And acting like a nutter
It's 'cause my insides are wiggly wobbly
And all in a flutter!

But... you can imagine my relief
As I stand here and chat
That it wasn't a blue bottle
But a harmless little gnat!

WHAT THE DUST?!

As I vacuum my carpet
For the umpteenth time
I ask myself how can dust
Get under this rug of mine

It's like someone comes at night
With a silent spray
Emitting particles of dust
For me to find the next day

I always wear slippers or socks
So don't understand
Why there's more dust in my house
Than the Gobi desert has sand

The more I vacuum
The more I find
But how it gets under my rug
Is baffling my mind!

SLEEPLESS IN BEDFORD!

I toss and turn
Most of the night
First to the left
Then to the right

On my back
Like an Egyptian Mummy
Curled up like a foetus
Knees up to my tummy

Thinking 'bout my diary
And all the t'do's
Thinking 'bout those passwords forgotten
Even though I have the clues

Who would've imagined sleeping
To be such a chore
Fidgeting so much
That the duvet's on the floor

My pillows too
Have gone the same way
It's gonna be a challenge to not dose
For the whole darn day!

ALL IN A DAY!

I started in Liverpool
Travelled to Poole
No waiting In line for my ticket
Man, how cool!

Onto Cornwall and Bristol
And my energy's still high
Then to Chester and Oxford
And Ross-On-Wye

I'm enjoying the scenery
Taking in the view
The history of each town
Is eye opening too!

I'm going to Edinburgh
The Castle's a wow!
Each room's so majestic
I could move in right now

My kind of vacation
Travelling light
No traffic or heavy luggage
Or driving at night

Great value for money
And it didn't break the bank
The safest way to go on holiday
And I have my tv to thank!

BE NOT MOVED!

I want to stay in bed
And watch tv
Make myself a sandwich
And a herbal green tea

Do nothing other than chat
On the phone to mates
And catch up on the programmes
I'd previously taped

And, if anyone comes knocking
Be assured I will not
Be answering or moving
From this comfortable spot!

NEW BEST FRIEND!

A good job I was early
'Cause when I re-checked my face
I found my lipstick had travelled
I was such a disgrace!

My cheeks were smudged red
And my snout, the colour of a rose
Looked more like I'd stolen
Rudolph's nose

A mirror's not normally
My ultimate friend
But today I was thankful
For this accoutrement no end!

WHAT'S ON YOUR PAVEMENT?

A fizzy drink can
A child's right shoe
Some selfish dog owner
Who's not cleared up its pooh

Plastic bottles once filled
With water or drink
Overfull wheelie bins
That absolutely stink

An old t-shirt
A broken chair
The remains of a takeaway
The stench of which fills the air

Cigarette ends
Used face masks
Stuff what shouldn't be there
You know, so don't even ask!

A child's old car seat
Baby wipes and tissues
Cotton buds, plastic containers
Bits of wood that can't be reused

Who are they
With the brain disability
To dispose of rubbish
Responsibly

Littering our streets
Making them unclean
They should be caught and deported
To where they can't ever be seen!

ALL TOE EGO!

One question I keep asking
Looking at my toes
Is if they all have the same food
Why the middle one grows

Longer than the big one
And the other three
There's no logical reason
That I can see

They all walk the same distance
At the same time each day
All get the same rest and relaxation
And are pampered in the same way

So, why one will grow
Exceedingly bigger
For the life of me is an enigma
I cannot figure

If anyone has any reasoning
Why this should be
Then I'd be grateful if this information
Was explained to me

But I hope in this area
The growth procedure has stopped
'Cause I'm running out of my supply
Of unholy socks!

A GOOD SNOUT!

I appreciate my nose
No, really it's true
It's surprising how grateful one is
When it doesn't work as it should do

It started with pepper
I sprinkled when cooking
But I was a little heavy handed
And wasn't looking

I breathed it in
While shaking the can
And the grains went into
That nasal cavity – oh man!

I sneezed and sneezed
And was well aware
That something quite fatal may happen
If I didn't catch air

Thankfully I managed
During a short reprieve
To sip some water to stem the bout
I was so flipping relieved

So, I shall learn from this moment
When the pepper's in hand
To keep a safe distance 'tween said
condiment
And where I may stand!

ONCE A CHILD ALWAYS A CHILD!

At five the days
Went on forever
And Friday's steak
Seemed as tough as leather

At seven I thought
I was almost grown
But I still wasn't allowed
To use the 'phone

At fifteen – an adult
I could do as I choose
But whatever I asked
Was constantly refused

Twenty one – oh good
The key to the door
I didn't know it meant things
Would be worse than before

And now? Little change
Though I have my own home
I still can't chew steak
And I don't think I'm grown!

THE WHISTLEBLOWER!

Whistling's okay
When it's just you
But walk round a supermarket
Listening to that hullabaloo

Constantly like a mosquito
Buzzing in y'ear
You either feel to punch the warbler
Or shed a frustrating tear

Walk down any aisle
One can hear the strain
Of that caterwauling slowly
Driving you insane

A rule should be in place
And the culprit subjected
To a playback of his whistling
Audibly injected!

Another solution perhaps
To possibly stop this din
Is to buy a 20p shopping bag
To stick his head firmly in!

I DON'T LIKE DUMMIES!

Do they ever put dummy pockets
In clothes men wear
That are just for looks
Not to put stuff in there?

Do men need to carry
A bag like a case
When they're driving or commuting
From place to place?

Why do designers
Appear to assume
We girls enjoy carrying a bag
Like a mobile storeroom

Please give us ample pockets
For purse and pen
So we can travel uncluttered
Just like the men!

WHAT A MARVEL IS MAN!

I could sit all day watching
Planes come and go
Ascending fast
And coming down slow

It's a miracle how man can design a car
A truck, a bus
But to get a plane to stay up in the sky
Is nothing short of gen–i– us!

PEACE PEACE GLORIOUS PEACE!

You go on holiday
I'll stay indoors
You can spend time queuing
I'll catch up on all my chores

Enjoy your traffic jams
The variable speeds while you drive
Which makes you wonder going that slow
If you ever will arrive

You enjoy the crowds
Me, the peace and quiet
You indulge in what treats you like
I'll just stick to my diet

You'll enjoy your break away
Where the sun'll constantly shine
And the tranquility here at home means
That I'll definitely enjoy mine

I'll not stress on the thousands saved
By having my staycation
And I hope you'll be happy in debt
After your lovely sunny vacation!

THE PLEASURES OF TRAVEL?

Will I forever be surprised
By the sights I see
On tube, train or bus
Slap bang in front of me?

CRUSTS OFF!

Well, the weather's holding up
We've had a few days sunshine
And everyone's getting tanned
With the climate so fine

But folk mustn't forget
Now that legs are bare
It's all well and good
Shaving unsightly hair

But those crusty white patches
That on heels are seen
Need to be filed off then moisturised
With Vaseline or cream!

ALL FIRED UP!
(Trains of the 20th Century!)

This train is full
And it's only six-fifteen
It's going so slow, honestly
I could scream!

The temperature in here
Is getting quite hot
'Cause the windows are shut
And the doors are locked

But I'm so thankful
That I have a seat
'Cause I'd probably have passed out
Because of the heat!

TRAINS, WHERE?
(trains of the 20ᵗʰ Century)

The trains are still
Up the spout
It's enough to make anyone
Scream and shout

It's not enough that they're dirty
Filled with rubbish and gum
Now they've revised the timetable
So some of 'em don't even run

We've paid our fare
To be packed like sardines
With someone's armpits in y'face
That's not smelling too clean

'Twas no different last year
They strike, win and are pleased
And we suffer the consequences
As the fares are increased!

Has anything changed today? I wonder!

RICH PICKINGS!

I raised my hand
In mild disgust
Squeeze that spot
If you really must

But I wish you'd do it
In a secret place
So that I don't have to see you
Pick your face!

MORNING STENCH!

This fellow came in
And he stunk of smoke
He smelled so high
I thought I would choke

He was smoking on the platform
And drinking beer
But how did I know
He would sit so near

By the end of the journey
I really do think
That it's not just him who'll be smelly
I too will stink!

FIRST THEN SECOND WISH!

I watched the plane in the sky
As it faded away
Taking excited passengers
On holiday

I looked up again
It was no longer in view
How I wished I was up there
Going on holiday too!

But then I thought – no!
Thinking of all the time
I would have to spend
Queuing in line

Then after many a sacrifice
To save up then be told
Matters not if you booked in advance
Or the plane ticket sold

Your scheduled flight
For which payment was made
Has now been cancelled
Not slightly behind or even delayed

I'm certainly glad
My hard earned cash
Is still with me and not part
Of any airline company stash!

QUIET TIMES!

It's quiet now
Such a joy
It's warm, the train's empty
There's nothing to annoy

The peace I am feeling
Whilst absorbing the view
The journey's the same
There's nothing new

But it's uninterrupted and soothing
And surprisingly I find
Very relaxing
And calming for the mind!

WHERE'S THE TRAIN....
WHERE...IS...THE...TRAIN?!

The train waits for no man
So when you see me coming
Don't stand in my way
Or obstruct me when I'm running

I have to catch my train
'Cause the next one might just be
Late through leaves, signals or cancelled
Or delayed permanently!

ONE OF THE MANY WONDERS OF OUR LAND

Beauty in petals; My new found love of flowers has me completely dazzled by their fragile beauty.

I look at each one and they never fail to make me smile – they are gorgeous – as are my mates, whose gardens they allowed me to wander around taking pictures – thank you! –

You may find a petal or two dotted around the pages of this book to induce a smile!

It only takes one flower to make a smile!

A SUNFLOWER FOR YOUR DAY!

Hope you find
Your day is as bright
As this sunflower is
Both now and at night!

THANK YOU MY FRIENDS!

The friends I have
Are lovely, they're kind
The friends I have
Are never far from my mind

We met by chance
It was never planned
Unless it was pre-arranged
By His Blessed Hand

And t'was on His radar
So was destined to be
That sooner or later
You'd all be friends with me

A gift from God
Is each friend of mine
And I pray this will be the case
From this day, for all time

READ AND SMILE!

As I wrote this verse
And signed my name
The flowers made me smile

And as you read I hope
It makes-you-do-the-same—too
At least for a little while!

PETALLIC BEAUTY!

That serenity in a petal
Has a certain amount of charm
The beauty one gets by looking
Emits a certain sense of calm

Though it won't discount one's pain
Won't eliminate your grief
The beauty in a flower
Will almost certainly bring you peace!

SIMPLE CAN BE BEST!

Isn't it awful
When you don't feel well
Whether physical or emotional
It hurts like hell

You want to cry
But don't want to look weak
And you get so down
You can't bring yourself to speak

Then something so simple brings your mind
From that place so blue
And makes you forget
What was bothering you!

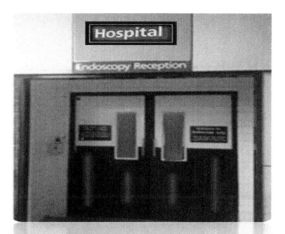

HOSPITALOSCOPY

'Tis an extremely healthy, fit and lucky person who has never had the experience of being treated in hospital. But for the lesser fortunate of us who've had broken bones, and other ailments requiring hospital attendance, necessary procedures are very rarely enjoyable!

An experience many, I am sure, probably have endured at some point on this earth, at least once!, hopefully never to be repeated!

Parts 2 and 3 are found later on in this book!

HOSPITAL EXPERIENCE NO 1 – A STICK UP!

Not another strange finger
Forced to the back
I pray I don't embarrass myself with
An unexpected air attack

For we all know 'tis human at times
To have air in y'gut
But not very ladylike to let it blow
In company from y'butt!

THE ROMANCE....
LET'S GET LOVING!

Whether in real life or not

Love, so they say, makes the world go round
But for some of us it seems
Love has gone deep underground
And we must be satisfied living in our dreams!

MY AGENDA!

I would pull you into my meeting
If I had the chance
And the agenda would be cuddles, kisses
Hugs and dance

We'd be in conference
Any day from early sun
And that consultation would last
Until day and night were done!

LIVE AND RELIVE!

I'm glad we have memories
And can turn back time
To that hour, and for that hour
When I was yours and you were mine

I'm glad we have our memories
And when you seethe from the day's trial
Remember that hour, turn back the clock
Close your eyes and smile!

TRAIN TRAVEL THINKING

And as I sit
Looking out at the view
My eyes may be focused on outside
But my mind's centred on you

My hands may be cold
And so too each toe
But thoughts of you just fill me
With an everlasting glow!

SECRETS!

Should feelings have to be explained
Or are they the unspoken word
Every emotion understood
Though nothing is ever heard

Are feelings a right
To be enjoyed or stored
And kept hidden away
Inside and ignored?

HAVE I TOLD YOU LATELY?

Have I told you lately
How much you're missed
How I long to be near you
How I long to be kissed?

Have I told you lately
Of the excitement that surrounds
My whole being whenever
You happen to be around?

Have I told you lately
Did I mention yesterday
Did you have any notion
That you affected me this way?

I NEED YOU!

Come hug me
To keep me warm
Shelter me from the world's
Tempestuous storm

Come kiss me slow
And tenderly
To ease the bruises
Others lay on me

Caress my body
To relieve the stress
That prevents my
Future happiness!

MY NUMBER ONE!

You top my list
Every day
With your sweet thoughts
And your gentle way

Top my list in more ways
Than I care to admit
And in my heart
You're definitely a hit!

SWEET PUNISHMENT!

You make my heart ache
With such sweet sweet pain
A sensation I'm happy to feel
Over and over again

Those moments of ecstasy
Is a pain so divine
That makes me a sucker for punishment
Every single time!

A FOOL TO LOVE!

Am I a fool to want you
Am I fool to pray
That we will be together
Hopefully some day

Am I fool to believe
Or is it so extreme
To wish for those things to be reality
Instead of just a dream?

NEW LOVE!

At first I never noticed him
But my heart did
Then my eyes realised
And my excitement went off the grid

He's lovely I thought
No, that's wrong
He's really gorgeous and my liking went
From weak to strong

Not that he's seen me
But my insides were like butter
I couldn't stop looking
I was all in a flutter

It's been a whole week
And my mind's eye can still see
That beautiful image standing
In front of me!

FOREVER MOMENTS!

I love when we're together
But hate when you leave
Because I'm left alone again
To lament and grieve

And constantly reminisce
On the times that we've shared
The good, the sad
When you've been there when I've been scared

If I could pick a time
To again go through
It would be all those moments
I've spent with you!

ALWAYS IN A DREAM!

The excitement I feel
As the time gets near
When work will finish
And you'll be here

Is like no other
But I know some'll say
That I only saw him
Yesterday

But for me each moment
I spend with you
The whole experience
Feels brand new

And all my dreams
Start over afresh
Ensuring each day I live's filled
With happiness!

THE WEIGHTING GAME!

I will never understand how weight, food and exercise all work against me and the fat just piles on, and on, and on.....!

EAT, DRINK BE MERRY
OR JUST BE HEALTHY!

GIVE ME FOOD!

I look in my fridge
And I've nothing to eat
Oh, sure, there's food
But nothing sweet

My cupboard's not bare
But I can't find a food
That's not veg or spice
To enhance a good mood

I've chocolates and cake
Biscuits and crisps
Enough crackers to dunk
In umpteen dips

But the sugar contained
And saturated fat
With the doctor's scowl means
I can't eat any of that

So, as I search my kitchen
In rather sombre mood
I realise we eat to maintain life
And not to enjoy food!

WEIGHTS AND PLEASURES!

Now, If one doesn't each chocolates
Hardly ever eats sweets
Rarely buys takeaways
Cakes, desserts or treats
If one's menu each day
Barely includes meats
Then why does one put on weight?

If one's always doing exercise
In one form or another
Walking, running, sports, DIY
And the regime only gets tougher
And the only payback you can see
Is that you regularly suffer
How come one still puts on weight?

I eat spinach, beets, and watercress
And enough celery sticks
To put hairs on y'chest
I eat lettuce, cucumber
Sugar snap peas
And broccoli spears
That resemble miniature trees

Carrots, kale – I could go on for weeks
Apples, grapes, lychees, leeks
Every fruit that grows on trees
Every veg growing under these
Finds its way onto my plate
And down the hatch at an alarming rate
And yet I increase in weight!
Hmmmm!

Maybe it's cakes and veg
That's making me fat
So, what if I stopped eating all of that
And substituted puds and cakes instead
Ice cream, cheese and white sliced bread
Meats, sauces and creamy spreads
Then, would I......could I...Be slim like you?

GOOD AND BAD IN ONE!

Far be it for me
To be so bold as to question
Any of man's
Or a higher being's invention

But I dare anyone to admit
They absolutely like
The texture of a pomegranate
When they take a bite

It may be a nutritional
Fruit to eat
But couldn't the inventor have added
Less pips and more meat

If it must have pips
In every bit
Why could they not have been soft
Instead of tasting like grit

It ain't easy to enjoy
And it's a challenging feat
Trying to savour the taste
With them pips 'tween y'teeth

I suppose we must suffer the bad
To get the good
But I'd far rather do justice
To an apple pie pud!

THE WAITING GAME!

I'm waiting for my body
To consume its own fat
Then my tummy and thighs
Will be super super flat

Though my intake of food's less
With every waking day
It's not affected my blubber
In any significant way

It's been quite some time now
And though I no longer feel bloated
What should be skin and bone
Is still heavily fat coated!

I'm convinced it's in my genes
So when the nurse comments on my weight
I shall waste no time at all
In putting her straight!

MORE IS LESS!

I eat more fruit
Walk twice as many miles than before
And yet society says
We should eat less and exercise more

All the foods we consume
Contain less sugar, less fat
And yet I get larger
Now how do you figure that?

Moving to decimal
Must take some blame
For food sizes getting smaller
And the price staying the same

With all these changes
Please be frank
And explain why the only thing smaller
Is the money in my bank!

GIMME, GIMME GIVE ME!

Sometimes I just need
A bit more on my plate
Some days lettuce and tomatoes
Won't sustain this weight

It could if I was losing something
Other than hope
But a size zero on me
Isn't in sight – no siree – nope!

Just give me something
Which will justify the labour
Of chewing food that's palatable
And not tasting like paper

That's not detrimental
To my health
And can be eaten with minimal preparation
By myself

Something either savoury
Or a little sweet
Not tasting like sawdust
Or chewy to eat

Not like straw
Or hippo skin
But succulent, tasty
And an absolute sin!

A GOOD SNIFF!

I'm not sure I'm hungry
But yet I could eat
And, if I don't have an early lunch
Then I'll have to have a treat

The smell passing houses down the road
With their lunch filling the air
I think can I knock on their door
And ask "Do you have some to spare"

From the aroma of a roast dinner
To a rhubarb and apple pie
It's enormously enticing
To my insatiable mind's eye

But, by far the best of all
Which never fails to please
Is the whiff of fish and chips
With a topping of melted cheese!

TOO BIG FOR MY TUM!

Oh no! I've overeaten
I knew I would
I really shouldn't've had
That second pud!

My eyes are way
Too big for my head
At this rate I'll never lose
The amount of kilos the doctor said

But it was too yummy to leave
And put in the bin
'Cause to waste anything nowadays
Is an unforgiveable sin

So, yes, I stuffed it down
And didn't stop
Until I had scooped up
The very last drop

And now the painful consequence
Has begun
And I'm here uncomfortably nursing
A very tender tum!

CHICKEN, EGG, EGG, CHICKEN?

What came first
Micro chickens or micro eggs
Have you seen the tiny sizes
Of chicken wings and chicken legs

Where are the adults
I continuously cry
The ones I remember
My mother used to fry!

Modern day chickens
Are bone and skin
And nothing but the container
And plastic packaging

But I must buy what they sell
Since they're better for you
'Cause they contain less fat
Than the other meats do

But I do so wish
The percentage of meat
Was more than the bone and skin
That I can't eat!

Eat me.....EAT ME!

When is my stomach gonna shrink
To half its size
Has it not noticed
Does it not yet realise

The smaller portions
I'm having to eat
Drinking sugarless beverages
And even less satisfying treats

If I'm barely eating
Then I can't get bigger
Oh, tell me when will my body eat me
So I can be thinner!

HOSPITAL EXPERIENCE NO 2 – BEDSIDE PREP FOR PHOTO SHOOT

As I lie here on this bed
Watching the rain
Trying to calm my nerves
And not think of the pain

I do so want to run
And not return
To this situation that's making
My stomach churn

As I lie here thinking
Of the pain and my fear
It increases as the nurses chant
"Relax my dear!"

I want so to ask "Are you stupid?
Have you experienced the pain to come?
You lie relaxed while a camera's shoved up
Inside y'bum"!

REVIVAL TIME….

We all need at some point in our day to review, restock and replenish so….Let's lay back close our eyes, breathe in, ponder and chill!

TRANSPORTER!

I can look at a picture
And transport my being
Into whatever landscape
I am seeing

I can go and hide
And feel the breeze
Intertwine myself
In the safety of the trees

I can stay for as long
As I want or need
Meander slowly
Or at great speed

Taking time out
To ponder and chill
Much better than any
Therapy or pill

And when I'm ready to leave
'fore you count to three
As I look away from the picture
I'm back on the settee!

TWO MILES AWAY
BUT POLES APART!

How peaceful the land
When no one talks
You can relax y'mind
And collect y'thoughts

Unjumble, unravel
And sensibly assess
What is useful to keep
And what's nothingness

With the sky so still
And a gorgeous blue
The clouds fluffy white
Just make me go "Ooooo"

Oh to stay away from the City
With it's continual hum –
This quietness is calming
I'm composed and having fun

But alas I must leave
Reality won't wait
True life needs me to return
And participate!

YOUR SPACE!

When you find that happy place
Just stay awhile and own the space
Close your eyes and let that glow
Warm you up from head to toe

It matters not what chores
You have to do
Sit and enjoy that feeling
Running through

And if you feel you're not
Completely warmed up
Let nothing
Let no one interrupt

While you find and satiate yourself
With wholesome air
Filling your being
With a sizeable share

Now, open your eyes
And let your grin
Radiate from outside
And permeate within!

JUST SMILE!

When your spirits need lifting
Just stop and say
Nothing and no one's gonna stop me
From smiling today

It won't solve your problem
We know that for sure
But the frown on your face
Will be no more!

MY CHILL PILL!

They quietly graze
Unaware
That they keep me calm
Like the cold winter air

My mind is still
I feel at ease
As I sit and watch the sheep
I am at peace

The leafless branches
Dance in the air
To the tune of the winter breeze
Without a care

They move just enough
For a gentle sway
Not too much that they snap
And fall away

The undulating hills
The trees, the sheep
It's so relaxing I feel
I could almost sleep!

FIND IT!

No matter how rough
No matter how grey
One can still find something to make
A brighter day!

HOSPITALOSCOPY OF LIFE Pt 3 – THE PHOTO FINISH!

'Tis done!, 'Tis done!

Amen 'tis done
With hole in gown
To expose my bum

Embarrassed – maybe
And not at all fun
But amen 'tis done
Amen – 'tis done!

Though nervous, was calm
It never mattered
It only took minutes
Before they all were gathered

Surgically prepped
And suitably confined
Was I ready to expose
An overweight behind?

But in an instant
As quick as was revealed
Photoshoot over
Then all eagerly concealed

Just a questionnaire to complete
Then said visit will end
But one question asked was
Would you recommend this procedure..
to a friend!!
Dah!

WHAT'S IN A YEAR?

(Harvest, Remembrance, Christmas)

The festivities in each year that cause us to be thankful, recall with sadness or party are each in turn attended with gratitude, tears or excitement ......

THANKS FOR MY MEAT, TWO VEG 'ND PUD!

I do like gardens
The gardening – not so much
I just don't have
That green fingered touch

And, if harvest from our gardens
Was all on which we had to survive
I know for sure, today
I definitely would not be alive

For the dandelions and ragweed
Could not sustain
Even my little, but active,
Pea-sized brain

And, yes, I've planted
Oh, how I've tried
But any fruit and veg yield
Was sadly denied

So, for the gift given
To the chosen ones
To till the ground
To fill our tums

To those farmers who know
Just what to do
So food's in plentiful supply
For me, for you

For the shepherds and cattlefarmers
Whose livestock we use
For our Sunday roast
And midweek stews

We're all very appreciative
And may you from above
Be showered continually with blessings
Of harvest, of love!

DAILY THANKS TO THEM ALL!

For those who fight wars
Again and again
The girls and boys
The women and the men

Who risk their lives
Year upon year
In foreign countries
Despite their fear

Let's not just remember them
Once annually
But give thanks whenever we pray
For their continual bravery!

IT'S CHRISTMAS!!

OCTOBER CHRISTMAS!

Christmas now starts in October
Before gunpowder treason and plot
Harvest hasn't even been reaped
And we've not yet gathered in crops

The shops are now filled with Santas
Oversized reindeers and lights
And, though we all have more than plenty
We still try to buy everything in sight

Let's get through a time of Remembrance
And see Guy Fawkes up in flames at least
Before unpacking our baubles and tinsel
And planning our Christmas Day feast

I'd like a couple more months to save up
Before the mad rush is unavoidably here
And to prepare for the festive season
Of merriment, goodwill and cheer!

CHRISTMAS HERE WE COME!

Let's get Christmas off
To a cracking start
Let's not get flustered, but stay calm
T'keep oxygen pumping round the heart

Cool, collected
Gather our thoughts
On what needs to be prepared
And what needs to be bought

Whether we worry or not
Christmas won't care
If you're rushing around
Pulling out your hair!

So, embrace the preparations
Enjoy and have fun
The long queues, the traffic
The cold winter sun

The dwindling bank balance
The tired feet
The long hours traipsing
The busy city streets

Keep that smile on y'face
The countdown has begun
And don't stop smiling
'Til all Christmas Carols have been sung!

A WARM WELCOME!

I welcome Christmas
With a warm embrace
'Cause the lights and decorations
Do wonders for this place

All we need now
Is the picturesque snow
Rudolph, the sleigh
And Santa's Ho Ho Ho!

LOOKING FORWARD!

I'm looking forward to Christmas
I can't wait to see
All the decorations, the lights
The Christmas tree

I'm looking forward to Christmas
And basking in its cheer
That never ceases to accompany Christmas
Every single year!

LET'S HAVE CHRISTMAS!

A familiar scene
From which we never tire
The decorations, the trees
Stockings hung by the fire

Outside the roads
Are all aglow
The rooftops and pavements
Glisten with snow

The children eager
Too excited to sleep
Begging their parents
To stay up and peep

To see Santa
On his sleigh
Bringing presents to open
On Christmas Day

May your Christmas Day
And New Year see
Nothing but good
For your family!

ARE WE THE SAME?

Does Christmas mean the same to you
As it does to me?
The putting up of decorations
Decorating the tree?

Wrapping loads of presents
For friends and family
Does Christmas mean the same to you
As it does to me?

Do you do the same at Christmas
In your home as do I?
Preparing a much too large a turkey
And dozens of mincemeat pies

Making sure that everything
Is pleasing to the eye
Do you do the same at Christmas
In your home as do I?

Do you visit the same places I do
When Christmas time is here?
Visiting friends and wishing them all
Festive seasonal cheer?

Attending services in prayer and thanks
For Christmas and New Year
Do you visit the same places I do
When Christmas time is here?

HERE WE GO AGAIN!

Some will realise
They've left it too late
To order their turkey
For that all important date

We'll re-learn our carols
Ready to sing
In remembrance of that happy day
Of the birth of our King

As we deck the halls
And dress the tree
And prepare our celebrations
For friends and family

Be merry, stay safe
And keep going the festive cheer
Not just for Christmas
But throughout the New Year!

WANTED – A WHITE CHRISTMAS!

I don't know 'bout a White Christmas
'Cause all I've seen
Are shrubs and bushes
That are mostly green

There's been very little frost
And I really don't know
If this year we shall
Have any snow

How will Santa
Park his sleigh
To deliver all those presents
On Christmas Day

What will his reindeers think
When they're parked in the street
Without any frost
Ice or sleet

It'll be safe for us
Who have cars to ride
But a sleigh on clear roads
Will be hard to slide

So, I'll be pleased if just
For Christmas Eve Night
I wake up and see
That all is white!

LET'S NOT FORGET!

Let's not forget
What Christmas means
It's not just parties
And snowy scenes

Let's not forget
Why Christmas comes
It's more than just reconnecting with
Long time chums

Let's not forget
Why Christmas is here
It's more than just best wishes
And seasonal cheer

Let's not forget
What the Good Book says
So, for Jesus, for Christmas
Let's give thanks and praise!

AND

WHAT WOULD

THE KIDS SAY?

I'VE BEEN GOOD SANTA!

I'd love to see
Where Santa lives
And thank him sincerely
For the presents he gives

And I'd love to show him
How good I've been
I've not been selfish
I've not been mean

To show him how
I've helped my friends
To tell him I'm grateful
For whatever he sends

I hope that Santa
Will be pleased with me
And send lots of gifts
To put under my tree!

I SHALL SHARE MY DINNER!

I don't know what Santa's
Reindeers eat
So I'll leave some sausage rolls
No pastry – just meat

But for Rudolph with
His nose so red
I shall leave a hot
Mince pie instead!

SANTA SIGHTING!

I had a long nap
Earlier on
So I could stay up when normal
Bedtime had gone

I shall hide behind the sofa
So I don't get caught
Checking all the presents
That Santa has brought!

SKINNY SANTA!

I went to the market
And guess what I saw
Santa's sleigh
But I wasn't quite sure

'Cause the Santa I glimpsed
Looked very lean
And I didn't see any
Of his reindeer team

But I hope he's ready
'Cause I want to play
With some brand new toys
On Christmas Day!

HIS SPECIAL NOSE!

I wonder how Rudolph
Acquired his nose
Was it specially ordered
Do you suppose?

Is it red
Because it's hot
Or is it just
An inflamed spot?

Would he choose
To give it back
And exchange for one
That's brown or black?

I hope he doesn't
'Cause without his red nose
Would be like Santa with no beard
Or red and white clothes!

OH......IT'S FINISHED!

Christmas is over how was yours?
Mine was good
I had turkey and cake
And lots of Christmas pud

I had lots of presents
On Christmas Day
But the best was all the wrapping
It was fun to play

I went to church
And sang some songs
Well – I couldn't read the words
But hummed along

Mummy's taken the tree down
And switched off the lights
We won't have a tree
Any more to shine bright

She's cleared all my wrapping
From off the floor
I can't make a scrunchy noise
Now Christmas is no more

She's collected the cards
That sat on the mantle
Putting away the half used
Christmas scented candles

All the decorations
Are now put away
Until Santa comes on the next
Christmas Day!

APRÈS CHRISTMAS!

Does your Christmas finish on Boxing Day, or does it continue for a bit longer, quite a bit longer....

CHRISTMAS REMAINS!

I'm still vacuuming up Christmas
The tinsel remains
Also glitter from the silver stars
And decorated paperchains

Balloons that lost their air
And had fallen from grace
Now lay lifeless on my carpet
Now creating waste

Yes, still vacuuming those memories
That each year Christmas makes
Seeing friends and family
Baking festive cakes

The debris may be discarded
But not so each memory
Of carols sung, of hot mulled wine
Of the decorated Christmas Tree

Let each happy thought continue
To fill your heart with cheer
So every day is filled with a smile
To last throughout the year!

COMING DOWN!

My decorations came down
In military style
Same colours in one place
All neatly filed

Batteries extracted
So Santa and the like
Are immobilised and safe
Until the next Christmas night

But my cards are still up
So too my balloons
And I still enjoy playing
Some Christmas tunes

My mind still sings
The Nativity
And Away in a Manger
Is still with me

I'm hurting no one
I'm not in harm's way
What does it matter
If I'm not over Christmas Day

If it makes me smile
Outside and within
Then I'll keep them up to maintain
A Christmassy grin!

STILL CHRISTMASSY!

My balloons are still up
Adorning my home
And as long as they've air
I'll leave them alone

'Cause each time I see them
I stare awhile
And remember back to Christmas
And it makes me smile

And if it can do that
And makes me grin
Then keeping them up
Is a very good thing!

CHRISTMAS PLEASE STAY!

I don't want Christmas
To go away
My cards are still up
To this very day

Father Christmas is on a train
In the downstairs hall
And two reindeers stand beside him
Leaning up 'gainst the wall

There's a santa on a shelf
With an over-full sack
Of toys he must unload
Before he goes back

I want Christmas to last longer
Than its seasonal break
Though I can't stomach one more mince pie
Or Christmas cake

But give me the smiling faces
And the seasonal cheer
And let it carry on through every month
In fact, the whole year!

FIRST ENCOUNTERS OF THE FOUR LEGGED KIND!

I adore my mate's pets; furry, cuddly, funny – to their pets, passed and present, thank you!

DOGGONE!

Don't get me wrong – I like dogs but

I can't have one with a face
Bigger than mine
With two bulging eyes
Watching me all the time

And, when it's pleased
And wants a treat
He grins with teeth bigger
Than Bigfoot's feet!

I do love dogs
But none that'll shed
More hairs than I have
Growing on my head

Truly, I do love dogs
But I won't be outdone
By their four legs 'gainst my two
When we go for a run!

CANINE CURE!

Now, I grew up fearing
Man's best friend
But one chance meeting
Brought all that to an end

When confronted with a greyhound
That reached your waist
There's no time for fight or flight
And my heart just raced

When his mother assured: "He's okay
He won't harm"
I thought looking at those teeth
It's hard to stay calm

But as was said
Her words rang true
Dearest Smudge for curing my fear
My thanks goes to you!

MY NEIGHBOUR'S PET!

She, to my mind was
The coolest cat in the street
Had the softest fur
And, in short, was just plain sweet

She adored her mother
So gentle was she
They would sit together when at home
Watching tv

Wherever her mother went
She followed behind
Never out of sight
Always in mind

Even when she became unwell
She was still affectionate and cuddly
Dearest Jessica
You were absolutely lovely!

ENDLESS JOY!

My sister's dog
Is such a treasure
And I know she gives her mum
Hours and hours of pleasure

She follows her around
Wherever she goes
She loves playing in the garden
Whenever it snows

Such a beauty -
With her soft curly hair
And warm brown eyes
Just like a teddy bear

With toy in hand
She won't go away
Until mummy stops work
And takes time to play

Who would be without
Man's best friend
Day in day out
The joy doesn't end!

ODE TO MAISIE!

She'll scamper around
Run carefree
Whether indoors or out
Will play endlessly

She'll come when you call her
Sit if you say
Obey your instruction
If you tell her go away

She adores her walks
But will adamantly refrain
From even going outside
If she sniffs a hint of rain

She's potty about chicken
And also her toys
And some more than others
She really enjoys

A man's best friend
Is what they say
And my mate's lovable pooch
Is a friend for every day!

ISN'T SHE LOVELY!

Quiet yet playful
You'd be her friend
If you have a piece of string
She would play no end

With her brother and sister
Not a meow, not a sound
An air of calmness – Minimum
A bundle of joy to be around!

MY TYPE OF FUDGE!

A cuddly big ball of fur
She thinks she's a pup
Always ready to play
And won't give up

Her come-play-ball-with-me-eyes
Are hard to ignore
But she'll play until
You're tired and sore

With ball in mouth
She'll place at your feet
And'll wait patiently until
You admit defeat!

I don't normally like fudge
But this one I adore
When she gives affection and you give back
She'll just give you more!

OUR EVER CHANGING WORLD – OR NOT!

I sometimes wonder whether anything has been learned from past history, or whether all changes are for the better?....

WOULD IT?

Would it be so bad if the world
Had nothing to report
If thieves stopped stealing
And wars came to a halt?

Would it be terrible
If there was no crime
And you could walk the streets
No matter what time?

Would it be so disastrous
If kindness ran rife
And you didn't have to worry
For the rest of your life?

If journalists found nothing
About which to write
Except good incidents about those
Who'd seen the light?

Would it really be so awful living
In a world like this
In peace and harmony
In heavenly bliss?

Would it?

NEW YEAR, SAME THING!

Each New Year
I continually say
Beg, plead
Fervently pray

That man will improve
That man will learn
Bad's not the way
And to good they will turn

But proof is seen
With each year gone
That man cares not
With how much he does wrong

As a child I couldn't wait
Until I was grown
For naughty adults to pass on
So we'd have a crime free zone

How was I to know
Each New Year would be the same
And there'd always be evil men
To give our world a bad name!

SURPLUS TO REQUIREMENTS?

Do I need a brain?
Maybe before
But in this twenty-first century
Is it required any more?

With computers and robots
I don't need to spell
Though, pre 2015 I think
I did it pretty well!

Multiply, subtract
Divide and add
I wasn't fantastic
But I wasn't that bad

Searching in the library
With no Google to help
I walked there just fine
And found the info by myself!

Learned the books of the Bible
Both old and new
But touch a key on the computer
And it can find all for you

When evolution removes that
Which you no longer require
What will replace
The medulla oblongata?

When machines fail to function
Who'll be to blame
When I need to make a decision
But no longer have my brain!

OUR WONDERFUL LAND!

What a wonderful world
In whatever season
All have their uses
For varying reasons

'Tis a beautiful land
From sunrise to sunset
No other planet has been found
That can match it yet

Our lush glorious land
Provides what we need
Only one thing makes it bad
And that's man's greed!

WHO KNOWS BEST?

When I was a child
I thought adults knew best
And that our parents knew better
Than all the rest

I thought adults everywhere
Knew wrong from right
Feared neither man nor beast
Whether on foot or in flight

And that when adults spoke
We kids should obey
And that from their instruction
We should never stray

But now as a big person
And I'm sure you'll concur
That some adults are even naughtier
Than we kids ever were!

THE YEAR THAT WAS 2022..

Feeling hot hot hot and dry dry dry!

First the virus, which is still with us, albeit less severe, and now we battle with intense heat and limited water – so we're warned, oh and don't forget the increases in the price of petrol!

And we will always remember this year for Our Queen's Jubilee and then her sad passing!

STILL IN THE WOODS!

We may not be in the thick
But we're not out of the woods
So we must continue
As we all know we should

It may not be as dense
But it is still about
So let's keep being careful
'Til the virus is finally out!

GIVE ME BACK SOME!

I think I want a refund
From the car tax I have to pay
With almost the whole of 2020 not driving
And what's happening today

With protesters voicing their opinions
And higher petrol prices seen
They soon might be protesting 'gainst
themselves
On matters that need to turn green

Since the only cars that will be running
Will be either fuelled by air
Or flying frantically in desperation
On the proverbial wing and a prayer!

NO PETROL, NO GOODIES!
So to the law of yin and yang...

There has to be a bright side
To the current dilemma we face
Yes cars might have to stop running
If petrol doesn't get cheaper in this place

But one upside is the cleaner air
And, another, since I can't go and buy
Is the amount paid on my food bill this month
Won't be at its usual high

But definitely the most beneficial to me
And maybe it is fate
With not shopping for goodies I like to eat
I'm almost certain to lose some weight!
Aren't I?!

HEATWAVE COOLER!

Oh to sit in a bath with cold water
And not get out
Until early autumn when
Hot weather's not about

In the absence of a swimming pool
I would keep perspiration at bay
I could do a puzzle, listen to music
And keep cool all day

I....don't.... Care!

I could be wrinkled like a prune
Or creased up like a pug
I wouldn't be getting out
Wouldn't be pulling the plug

Until we can walk
In comfort again
Without fear of sweat drown
Or the sun frazzling our brain

Yes, I could sit in a cold bath
And happily stay there
'Til this heatwave's over
And autumn's in the air!

COOL AT ANY PRICE!

As I open the fridge
And enjoy the freeze
I think perhaps I could fit in there
With a little squeeze

Stuff fruit and veg
Ice cream and butter
Chocolate, yoghurt
And all other edible clutter

My body needs a cool down
If it is to function
So from buying groceries of any ilk
I'm taking out an injunction!

With my curvy stature
I'll be okay
The excess body weight'll easily
Feed me each day

So, whilst staying cool
I should be thinner
I'm beginning to think this heatwave
Is a weight loss winner!

FEELING HOT HOT HOT!

Gosh! I'm hot, so hot
Summer's already taken its toll
If it's cold you can wear more
But in this weather you've no control

Some folk don't mind
If they glow from the heat
But as for me, this shiny look
Is never neat

Y'energy is drained
Y'mascara runs
And panda eyes are not the thing
When summer comes

Warm weather's really nice
If protected from the sun's rays
This heat's bearable for a couple
But not for seven days!

Y'clothes get creased
And it's hard battling
Temperatures that make y'face resemble
Pork with crispy cracklin'

If I glisten like this
After such a short time
Imagine the state of me
When summer's at its prime!

BRING ON THE WATER!

I've had my quota of water
And every glass was so nice
Boiled, filtered and completely chilled
Topped with tons of ice

A cup of tea we all know
May cool you down much better
But give me a glass of Adam's Ale
Even in less warm weather

Each mouthful I dutifully happily drink
From break of day 'til night
Is nothing but renewed, repeated
Utter sheer delight!

ARE YOU JOKING?

Is that it?
Is that all?
Only a few spots of rain
Is all I've seen fall

Those menacing grey clouds
Saw me run
From each store in a bid to get
All my shopping done

To get back home
And not be stalked
By the long awaited downpour
Of which they all talked

But after days of drought
It seems just a bit
No - a joke – a few drops of rain
Is this really it?

RAIN....RAIN WE NEED YOU NOW!

Reservoirs run low
Rivers are dry
Will it end soon
"We hope so"!, we all cry

When we get our downpour
I shall promise never again
To pull a frown or moan whenever
We are blest heavy rain!

A ONCE WAS!

This once was a stream
Where water ran
Now it's steeped in debris
Plastic bottles, tin cans

How long will it be
Before the rain
Falls enough for the stream
To flow again!

HOT, SOFT AND RUNNY!

My lipstick's gone soft
The vaseline is runny
I won't mention the "H" word
But this weather's not funny

I'm sure I must have "glowed" off
Half my weight
Then put on twice that much
'Cause of the cold water intake

But we have only just
A few months to go
Before we'll be plunged into the time
Of ice, sleet and snow

So let's revel in a few weeks
Of hot glorious weather -
All good things (as they say) come to an end
And this heat won't last forever!

QUEEN'S JUBILEE CELEBRATION
JUNE 2022

WHAT A QUEEN!

Every little girl's fantasy
A childhood dream
To be a princess
But to become a Queen

Can you imagine going to sleep
A happy little girl
Then to wake up being the owner
Of your own little world

Could you have coped
With such responsibility
Tasked with looking after a nation
Cannot have been easy

Playing with toys
Were now put away
You had a country to look after
You had to grow up straightaway

And now seventy years on
Just as beautiful and with a smile
So radiant as when you were
First our Queen, and little more than a child

We celebrate all you do, have done
Seen and unseen
We all thank you for your service
Long live our Queen!

A SAD FAREWELL!

(Thursday 8 September 2022)

Our Queen this day
Her time with us sadly at an end
Mother, Auntie, Grandmother
Great Grandmother, Friend

Much loved by Her people
Her loyalty, Her drive
Her determination and willpower
Whatever the circumstance to survive

Her absence from our lives
Will be felt by all
With this ultimate duty to answer
That final call

To Her family and friends
The finest Lady I've ever seen
Our thoughts are with you all at the passing
of
Your Mum, your friend, and
Our Gracious Queen!

FINAL GOODBYES!

(Monday 19 September 2022)

As we mourn the loss
And celebrate Her life
Look back on Her roles
As Monarch, Mother and Wife

As thousands flock
For their last goodbyes
Pay their respects
With tears in their eyes

We may welcome Your Son
Our King today
But memories of You, Ma'am
Won't ever go away!

IN WHAT/WHO DO WE/I TRUST

As years go on we may find we trust in less, or more, or different things, but one thing's for sure as humans we will have faith and trust in something, or things!

And, all creatures are welcome to congregate and share in whom one may trust!

HE'S NEVER FAR AWAY!

Whether the grass is green
Or the sky is blue
Whether the ground has snow
Or is wet with dew
Whether the sun is shining
On me and you
He's always there

Whether it's cold
Or whether it's hot
Whether one's rich
Or whether one's not
In a cool situation
Or a tight spot
He's always there

Whether you're in church
Or sat at home
In a crowd
Or on your own,
Whoever you are, child
Or fully grown
Remember – He's always there!

HEAVEN ON EARTH!

How to live in Heaven
Here on earth
Takes a lifetime of learning
From the moment of our birth

We have to learn how to forgive
Though we'll probably not forget
Learn how to manage bills
And not get into debt!

To smile through our sorrow
To laugh through all pain
To overcome anger and hatred
Again, and again, and again!

To have Heaven on earth – I've learned
And it's kept me going thus far
Is to have a steady flow of God's blessings
Cheese, music and a dependable car!

NO COMPARISON!

How can I compare
To the magnificence of the sky
The comfort of green fields
And graceful birds flying by

How can I compare
To the beauty all around
So majestic, so perfect
It continues to astound

How can I compare
To the love that You give
Your overall generosity
So that each of us could live

How can I compare
To the greatness of it all
I cannot compare
Not at all, not at all!

BEE IN CHURCH!

A bee came to church
A big one at that
It flew so near
It almost knocked off my hat

It swooped down so low
I bobbed just in time
To see it miss the Holy wafer
But dive into the wine!

Not sure anyone noticed
But I'm positive I heard the sound
Of something frantically desperately
Splashing around

The vicar seemed unperturbed
As he lifted the cup
I'm just watching intently to see
Whether he gobbles it up

I'm giving communion a miss
Well at any rate the wine
In case I swallow something
Less grapey and less divine!

FOREVER SUNDAY

If every day was Sunday
We'd be enjoying a Sunday roast
Not grabbing a quick biscuit
Or gooey cheese on toast

If every day was an at-church-day
I have a sneaky hunch
That some would be listening to the sermon
And others would be focused on lunch

If every day was a Sunday
We'd be relaxed on each day we see
Never at work but always getting paid
Spending every day praising Thee!

MORNING PRAYER!

Keep us safe by day
As You do by night
Let all we do be pleasing
In thy sight

Let your loving spirit
Surround us all
And from Your Grace Oh Lord
Please let us not fall

Bestow Your blessings on each
And everyone
From the end of one day
'Til the next one has begun

Let all we do
Think and say
Encourage all those we meet
In a positive way
Amen!

BE STRONG!

Let your faith be stronger
Than the difficulties you go through
Whether it be financial, medical
Or emotional for you

Let the strength of the conviction
In whom you place your trust
Overpower all negativity
Blowing it away like worthless dust

Then let sheer will and determination
Take over that place
And override whatever problem
Life compels you to face!

FEELING THE BLUES?

MUSIC'S THE CLUE!

LET MUSIC LIFT YOU UP!

No morning after hangover
No headache
No thumping feeling
When you awake

Just a sweet sweet sensation
Making you realise with a sigh
That when you're feeling down music
Will lift you high!

REAL SAXY!

Oh lovely saxophone
You're such a wow!
You're smooth and sexy
Let me play you now

Trim and beautiful
Great to hold
You may look like brass
But you're more precious than gold!

MUSICAL CLEAN UP!

How can a little 5ft1" girl
Produce so much clutter
I shall attempt to clear
Whilst listening to Rutter

Then to mix it up a bit
While cleaning the car
To easy singing from Bing
Like Swinging On a Star

While vacuuming the house
A touch of Tom Jones
Who doesn't know the words
To the Green Green Grass of Home?

I've hung the washing listening
To Cole Porter
And singing the words
Well, kinda, sorta

The carpet on the stairs
Gets a burst too
With Ole Blue eyes singing
Embraceable You

I've worn myself out
With singing as I clear
So it's in the corner for the vacuum
And in my hand, a beer!

PERFECT TONIC!

The only thing I have patience with is music

I am awed by its beauty
Warmed by its glow
And my admiration for its versatility
Can do nothing but grow

The only thing I fear not is music

It creates no wars
It knows no hostility
Recognises not discrimination
And abhors animosity

I have the greatest respect for music

It is soothing
When I am down
Always comes to the rescue
With its reassuring beautiful sound

*One thing unlikely to harm is music

Unlike meds this tonic
Only comes in one way
Through the ears
And relaxes as it plays

Doses can be taken
In small or large measure
And one can only overdose
With sheer pleasure

Yes, the only thing I have patience with
Is music!

FILL ME WITH MUSIC!

I'd rather play music
Than eat a meal
It's just as, if not more, satisfying
Without that bloated feel

I can regularly indulge
Umpteen times a day
No calorie counting
And nothing to weigh

I can overdo any jam session
And not be sick
Sure, my fingers might ache
But that's about it

I think that's the perfect
Dietary plan
So I'll play, play, play
As often as I can!

TUNEFUL TONIC!

I can rarely think of anything
Better to do
When smiley thoughts are far away
Or I'm sad and feeling blue

Than sitting at my keyboard
And banging out a tune
'Cause as the noise fills my mind
And every inch of the room

Those non-happy feelings
Are quickly transferred
Into happy vibes as if
Nothing sad had ever occurred

The best pick-me-up
That I can recommend
Is a good bang out session
'til those bad feelings end!

MY KINDA FOOD!

Music is like food
I can't do without
As long as I have music
I'll want for nowt

I'm not that choosy
Most anything will do
Classical, R&B, Gospel
Rock n roll too

A world without music
Seems an existence alone
That faint hum of beauty
To welcome you home

That up-beat din
To accompany your drive
That familiar tune that detracts
And keeps focus your mind

Where would I be without music?
I know exactly where
In a dark and dismal place
Where I've pulled out all my hair!

So I'll keep my music and avoid
Names I may be called
'Cause I'm certain without it
I'd most definitely be bald!

HAPPINESS IS....

When I listen to music
I leave this land
I've no debts, no bills, my diary's empty
I've nothing planned

I close my eyes
And mentally stroll
My stress levels decrease
As it calms the soul

It's kinda hypnotic
As each note hits each ear
The troubles of the world
Immediately disappear

I float in pleasure
From tune to tune
Whether it be Magic Moments
Wonderful World or Fly Me To The Moon..

Alas! The music stops
And I have to prepare
To return to the big wide uncompromising
World out there!

THE LONG PLAY!

I don't believe
I'm the only one
That plays 'til my fingers are sore
And my rear is numb

That when I began
The room was light
And now I'm finished
The day's now night

That when I started
I had a full gut
And now it's grumbling
As if my throat's been cut!

I wouldn't mind if practising yielded
A more competent me
Not aching fingers 'nd a rear that's as hard as
A pack of frozen peas!

WHAT'S UP WITH IT?

What is it with singing
That we can't leave it alone
Many of us think we can hold a tune
But all that comes out is a groan

What is it with music
That whenever we hear the sound
Our ears twitch our toes start tapping
Then we want to jump and prance around!

AND SO,

LET LIFE CONTINUE

Oops Not Again!

A BIT O' LIP!

I bit my tongue
You can't believe the pain
And I wasn't quick enough to stop chewing
And bit it again!

Now it's swollen
To twice its size
And to finish this meal
Would not be wise

But I'm ravenously hungry
And won't be phased by this blip
Ouch! Serves my right now I've gone and
bitten
The inside of my lip!

LIVE AND DEPRIVED!

It's ten to five
I've been awake since two
I've tossed and turned
I've been to the loo

Watched a programme I recorded
The previous night
Caught up on Neighbours
And the Price is Right

I got up, walked 'round
Fiddled with this, touched that
Jogged on the spot
To lose some of the fat

Jumped back into bed
Switched off the light
Hoping to sleep
For the rest of the night

......It's ten to five
And I'm annoyed to say
I've not slept a wink
But must now start my day!

206

ANTIFLY!

Oh those ants – those pesky ants
Bloomin' flying ants!

The heat's woken them up
They've got me going spare
On the ground, in the bush
They're absolutely everywhere!

Look at the space
Under the earth they've got
But they now want to invade the air
And fly around when it's hot

Do they not have eyes
Can't they see
That they're flying and bumping
Right into me

Up my nose, in my eyes
Even in my hair
Who gave them wings
To fly up in the air?

I have to hold my breath
And quickly walk
Please no one stop me –
And want to talk

For these creatures may not
Be able to see
But if I open my mouth you can be sure
They'll fly inside of me

I've heard of butterflies in y'stomach
But I definitely call time
At having flying ants
Inside of mine!

GOODBYE HUMANS!

Is talking to a computer
Proof of sanity
Or evidence of the start
Of the extinction of humanity

They send us messages
Do our chores
Change channels on tv
Open doors

Store our books
Do our sums
Keep us updated
On the shenanigans of our chums

Map our route
When we drive
From the beginning of our journey
'Til the time we arrive

They keep us abreast
And constantly aware
Warning us of speed cameras
So we take extra care

Can answer any question
We may pose
From the perfect way to brew tea
To shopping for a tiara for your nose

We don't need to think
But just continue to train
Computers to takeover and eliminate
All humans with brains!

THE WRONG LEAD!

Am I such a honey
Or just so sweet
That these black and yellow wingers
Will follow me to any street

Whether wasp, bumble
Hornets - I don't care
They seem to find me
No matter where

I'm told if one's near
Keep still, stay calm
They pose no threat
And'll do you no harm

But if you think I'm sticking around
To prove that point
You're wrong! I'll be the first one
Outa that joint

I won't delay my exit
When I hear that hum
I'll make a hasty retreat
Before the swarms come!

CAN YOU ROAR?!

There are probably quite a few of us who say
That we never snore
Like the sound of a young lion cub's
Gentle roar

Or the faint trickle of water
Struggling to maintain
An orderly drip via the sink
And down the drain

How many of us whose sinuses
Are always clear
Can claim nobody they know
Can say they ever hear

A snore like a grunt, whistle
Or pneumatic drill
A gentle vibration
Or short sharp shrill

So, when next you hear someone doze
In front the tv
And there's a sound like a train
Rushing towards your settee

Just make sure
Before you kick up a t'do
That the noise is coming from them
And not from you!

IF ONLY!

If Christmas on tv
Is the only time
We can expect happy programmes
Without violence and crime

Then let us hope
And fervently pray
That it's the Christmas season
Every day!

BE SAFE!

And now the ending
Of our day
There are three things
Oh Lord I pray

That family and friends
You'll safely keep
Free from harm
As they rest and sleep

That You'll keep all evil
From their door
Not just for this night
But for evermore

And when night brings forth morning
I'll continue to pray
That You'll protect them as they journey
On their way!
Amen

THIS IS IT…. (for now!)

Acknowledgement

To Barbara, Mary, Joyce, Joni, Suzie, Bernadette, Chrissie and Gladys for either sending me photos or tolerating me traipsing round their garden taking shots of their beautiful flowers – so so pretty!

Also to Beverly and Denise for their photo contributions; to my sister Lorna, Gladys, my brother Lloyd, Bernadette, Suzie and Beverly (again!) for sharing their lovely pets - much appreciated – they are all so gorgeous!

About AngieD

Born and bred in North London and Enfield, experiencing life in Essex before finally settling, for the time being, a little further north than Watford.

Who knew her first poem about a mynah bird would evolve, years later, into a whole host of verses?

Whether commuting into London or staying local, a writing book is never far away.

Whether it's her passion for music, love of cheese or appreciation that most things in life are beautiful or will bring a smile, it may be 2.00am or 2.00pm but if it is perceived, it will be documented!

And, with another year into the journey of life, AngieD's verses continue to spill out in rhyme and, sometimes, irregular form.

Her aim remains to be one of entertainment and to keep people smiling at the mishaps which plague her road to contentment but which shape her existence.

If it makes others smile, she is happy to continue in human error – not that she has much of a choice more often than not!

As the song says: "To dream the impossible dream...", her target along this path is to be able to afford a dog and any prospective vet bills but, since reality has failed to intervene, she is content with the kindness of friends and family and sharing the joy of their pets!

AngieD can be found at any given time somewhere in a dream, with writing book in hand – and, if that dream comes true she promises to abstain from eating cheese for a week!

So, to all potential readers she says: read, enjoy and smile!

And Now

Both the author AngieD and Selfishgenie Publishing hope that you have enjoyed reading this book and that you have found it useful. You can e-mail AngieD at **angied@selfishgenie.com**

Please tell people about this eBook, write a review or mention it on your favourite social networking sites.

For further titles that may be of interest to you please visit the Selfishgenie Publishing website at **selfishgenie.com** where you can join our mailing list so that we can keep you up to date with all our latest releases (or maybe that should be 'escapes').

Printed in Great Britain
by Amazon

15760934R00129